Life is About the Dance

Poems and Inspirations

Lisa Brown Ross

Published by:
Before You Publish — Book Press
P.O. Box 2074
Addison, Texas 75001

Edits & Cover Designs:
In House at Before You Publish — Book Press

Published and printed in the United States of America
Copyright © 2020 Lisa Brown Ross

First Edition
ISBN-13: 978-0-9747388-6-4

Brown Ross, Lisa
Life is About the Dance: Poems and Inspirations — First Edition

Life is About the Dance
Poems and Inspirations

Lisa Brown Ross

Life is About the Dance

Poems and Inspirations

Lisa Brown Ross

September 2020

Beloved Tonya!

What a joy it has been to meet you and plan Kim's wedding — a time filled with so much love. I pray that God blesses you always — beyond anything you can imagine.

#LoveBasedLiving

In His Grip,

Lisa

BeforeYouPublish Book Press
— We Publish Books —

ADDISON, TEXAS

Contents

Life is About the Dance

How God Shows Up in the Rhythms, Bends, and Twirls of Life

Introduction

My family is artistic and talented. My maternal great-grandmother, Annie Lewis, was a pianist and taught the town's elite white folks in Ruston, Louisiana, how to play. My maternal grandmother, Minnie Ruth Davis (Nanny), also played the piano. So does my mom. My mother's cousin, who we call, Uncle Delbert, is an accomplished jazz saxophone player. He actually got a small part playing in the orchestra in the movie, "Lady Sings the Blues." Dad knows almost every song written by B.B. King and even at 95-years-old, quotes the lyrics and pops his fingers. My sister is a vocalist and equity actor. I suppose it was no accident that some aspect of art would be present in my DNA.

I fell in love with music—all forms of musical expression, literature and dance—at an early age. My first collection of poems was published when I was in high school. When Mom took my sister and me to see Cab Calloway and Pearl Bailey at the Shrine Auditorium in Los Angeles for the production of *Hello, Dolly*, I was captivated. We had seats on the third row, and I think I smiled throughout the entire performance. My eyes lit up as Ms. Bailey strutted across the stage. The costumes and the music—oh my, how I believed that I too would perform in a musical one day.

Every Saturday morning Mom had a routine for Renata and me. We got up early and cleaned the house to the tunes of Ramsey Lewis, Tom Jones, James Brown, Johnny Mathis and the smooth melodic voices of Lou Rawls, Sarah Vaughn, and Dinah Washington. I still remember some of the lyrics too. Classics like Lou Rawls' "You'll

Never Find Another Love Like Mine" or Tom Jones' "It's Not Unusual." Miles Davis was a staple and Mom had every Aretha Franklin album ever recorded.

When I went away to college, I became a disc jockey to offset the costs. It was one of the best jobs of my life. During the early days of disco, I cut my teeth at KSET 99.5 FM spinning records from 6 p.m. to midnight. But it was at KTEP 88.5 FM that I fell in love with every aspect of jazz. "KTEP 88.5 FM, your jazz station…" rolled off of my lips like butter. I took classes and studied jazz. Thelonious Monk, Louis Armstrong, Billie Holiday, John Coltrane and Jean-Luc Ponty (to name a few) felt like friends. I loved radio and using sound to create imagery. I was surrounded by thousands of albums of jazz, rhythm and blues, classical and Top 40.

As I fell in love with music, it was dance that captured my soul. I wanted to be a ballerina and studied ballet as a minor at Texas Woman's University and later at the University of Texas at El Paso. It didn't take long to recognize that I was much too late to the game. The kind of training required to acquire prima ballerina status or to become a serious modern dancer begins in one's formative years–like eight years old, not eighteen. It was clear the classes Mom enrolled me in at the community center didn't quite fit the bill. I tried and tried but never graduated to toe shoes. Through much practice–and I do mean a lot–I mastered the plié, grand battement and jeté, and began a serious love affair with the barre. Still I was never chosen to perform. I didn't lament about it too much. I had records to spin.

I enjoyed the stretches and watched in wonder at jazz dance and flamenco performances. The rhythms and syncopations of movement took me to another place. When the Alvin Ailey Dance Company and Dance Theatre of Harlem came to TWU, I had an opportunity to participate in a mid-level class. I had some movements down but not perfected. In order to be considered worthy, a mastery of skill was absolutely necessary. Again, I was much too late to be considered as a serious dancer and after Mom said, "Honey, you'll never make any money dancing," (giving me two tablespoons of love with three of reality) I gave up my dreams to become a dancer. I'm grateful my fascination and respect for the art form remain.

After an extremely blessed career in public affairs, public relations and leadership development, and raising children, being married and caring for elderly parents, I see a stark, beautiful connection and juxtaposition in the art form I love so dearly and life itself. I see it in how God shows up and responds to our decisions, heartaches, joys and faith. The Holy Spirit ministered to my soul on how God shows up in the bends, dips and twirls of our lives. He meets us at the barre when it's time to stretch. He greets us at the crucible when you just can't take another turn.

I've learned that we indeed have a choice in how we show up to life. We can choose despair, or we can operate with grace and gratitude. The truth is that when we choose God, we are always victorious no matter the outcome. We get to choose hope, mercy, compassion, perseverance and grace. We get to choose, and then God shows up and blows our minds. The act of faith comes first, and He always wants us to choose Him. He will never force himself on His highest creation and when we do choose Him, He will show us "…great and mighty things, which thou knowest not." (Jeremiah 33:3).

"Life is About the Dance" is about love and love-based living. For, God so loved the world that HE poured everything into HIS creation and gave us HIS only Son. Love is staying close to what is sacred and dancing the vibes and rhythms of life with intention. Love-based living is our opportunity to choose love—no matter what the circumstances are, and no matter how it may look. Yes, we get to choose, and, why not? Love is absolutely and positively spectacular. Love teaches us the value of life. Love-based living is knowing we are instruments of God.

#LoveBasedLiving
#LifeIsAbouttheDance

Acknowledgements

One of the wonderments of life is how God shows up when we say yes to Him. It is impossible to move, flow and create without assistance. This body of work is possible because of the artists who've surrounded me with their brilliance, love, creativity and imagination. I'm inspired by art and it's the voices of those who also love art for which I am eternally grateful. I'm grateful for my husband, **John**, who always says yes to my projects and to that part of me that longs for expression. He understands my spirit-self that seeks after the heart of God, and the desire I have to illuminate His Word by using the gifts He has bestowed. John, too, is a most creative spirit. He has the ability to gaze at a piece of wood and then create something spectacular. I've marveled at what a man's man he is; structured and always controlled. That's his law enforcement bent. Yet, his imagination is bountiful and rich.

When God created my children, He did something pretty special. They keep me on my knees and always give me something to write about. They have taught me to surrender my will to God's will. **Jade-Lauren** believes her mother can move the wind around. **Joshua's** creativity and imagination are mind-bending. **Daniecia (Heaven)** provides a softness and kindness that makes me cry. **Biron** challenges me to think; **Kimon** teaches me about God's promises and to never, ever give up praying.

My sister, **Renata** is a rock—always there, no matter what. As an equity actor and vocalist, she's taught me to embrace the assignment God has given me.

My tribe's words of encouragement and inspiration provide me fuel to go further, reach higher and stretch myself. **Vivian** Phillips is the consummate arts patron, producer and director; a confidante, friend-for-life, and soul sister. The Word of God says that a friend can be closer to you than a brother/sister. **Sherel** Riley—that gal that I sling snot with—I go to her enormous capacity to love and am never disappointed. Sherel makes me better. **Teresa** Coleman-Wash encourages me to stretch and lean into my fears. In 2018, I did just that by partaking in the feast known as The Monologue

Project in New York City. And then, there are the prayer warriors who have me on their minds during that most sacred time of prayer. For more than 21 years **Mary** Bogan has mentored me in God's incredible Word. I have notes, letters, emails and journals with Mary's words of wisdom written and worn over the pages. When we talk, I take copious notes–**Kim** Powell, **Marsha** Sherrill, and **La Tanya** Harris. When it's time to ask God for heaven to rain down on earth… they are my go-to women, without fail, my prayer-warrior sisters who cover me and accept me as I am, ashy legs and all.

And then there are my "youngins" that God has given me to pray over, guide, encourage and inspire. My godbaby, **Stormi** Demerson is an uber-gifted actor, painter and poet. She helps me to rise. My phone has encouraging texts from her from two years ago. **Tiffaney** Dale, my other godbaby, continues to inspire me as she shows so much courage in the midst of her own personal storms. These "youngins" have become real women.

I have always said that good editors make good writing great. **Elaine** Garcia is a word-surgeon who edits with precision. I'm grateful for every revision. I would never put anything in the public domain without knowing that Elaine's eyes saw my work and her red pen had etchings on the pages. She has also become a trusted friend–my fierce sister in the revolution.

When I looked for help with the photos and pulling that piece together, there were only a few folks that I trusted with my vision. **Vicki** Meek responded immediately with suggestions. Her work in the creative space is legendary and I have major respect for her. **La Wonda** "La'Hunter" Hunter-Smith, former principal dancer for the Dallas Black Dance Theatre, has been an absolute jewel. Before I completed my pitch, she said yes. Her time and dedication are everything to me. I couldn't have kept the timeline without her. **Michelle** N. Gibson, MFA, is just a super bad choreographer, educator, and performer. I have mad-love and a full heart for the photographers and dancers who so graciously said, "Yes."

"Life is About the Dance" is a labor of so much love. I became pregnant with this body of work more than six years ago but some of the poems and essays go back 10 years. It wouldn't have happened without the gifts from those who gave of themselves so generously. I am forever grateful for the support and trust to take this baby from conception to birth. *Thank you.*

Dedication

To my husband, John, with whom I have danced through a life that has been filled both with unspeakable joy and heartbreaking turbulence. To my children whom I hope will learn to dance with vigor, love, and aplomb. To my sister, Renata who gives me reasons to dance, and to my mom and dad, Doris and Curtis Brown, who taught me to dance and are still dancing because…

Life is About the Dance

This photo was taken in 1964 of my sister Renata, our friend, Jimmy and me. We were invited to join Archie Bell and the Drells on stage at a concert in Kaiserslautern, Germany. The name of the song and dance we were asked to perform was "Tighten Up," and tighten up we did.

Then Miriam the prophet, Aaron's sister, took a timbrel in her hand, and all the women followed her, with timbrels and dancing.

Exodus 15:20

Arabesque

Life is About the Dance

It's about the tap, tap, tap
Wrap, wrap, wrap
And the wiggle room between
Notes C and G—
The sway into
Another day and
Into the arms of God.

Life is about the dance.

It's about the rhythm,
The flow of your heart
Connecting to the hips
And freeing your mind.
It's seeing the floor
All of it
And listening to the
Drums, wind
And violins in
Your head.

Life is about the dance.

It's about the twist,
Jerk and salsa
Of your soul—
The wearing out of
Your shoes

The liberty in movement
And open space of faith.

Life is about the dance.

It's about the clap, clap, clap
And beating of tambourines
Until the sun rises
And light shines
On our tomorrows.

Life is about the dance.

It's about stepping out,
Leaning in with bloody and bruised knees—
Pushing through and backing up
Falling down
And getting your strut
Crying until there are no more tears...

Life is about the dance.

It's about making a groove
When there's no sound
It's getting up and
Getting down when
No one is around
And standing on your feet
Without applause.
It's crafting moves out of nothing
And moving forward

Even when
You're the only one
Dancing.

Life is about the dance.

It's about the spin and twirl
Swinging out and swinging in
To old songs and new beginnings,
Grand battements
As high as you can.
It's stretching and being stretched
And drawing circles on the floor.
It's being thrown, picked, chopped,
Caressed and held close
It's having contractions and giving birth.

Life is about the dance
It's living
Life is about the dance
It's giving
Life is about the dance
It's belonging

Life is all about the dance.

24

The Barre

Ballet begins at the barre. The barre looks easy and simplistic but it's not. The stretch at the barre is intense and you KNOW you have stretched when you're done. It reminds me of how God stretches us beyond our capacity; beyond our capability to "think" we can get there. Yet, He provides for us. He provides the opportunity. He provides the ability to lean into it so that the stretch is meaningful and purposeful, not in vain. God stretches us so we can grow and get to the next thing, to the next stretch. There have been moments in my life when I actually said aloud, "Lord, I just can't do this. I can't." And, the Holy Spirit whispered to me, "Yes, you can. One more moment. One more day. Perhaps today wasn't a good day, but remember, '... Weeping may endure for a night, but joy comes in the morning.'" (Psalm 30:5)

The purpose of the barre is to lengthen muscles as well as strengthen them. Isn't that a wonderful translation for how God desires to stretch us? My dear friend and confidante, Mary, told me once, "Lisa, you must exercise your faith muscles." When your faith is grounded in God's Word, the turbulent circumstances around you don't move you because faith says, "Joy is coming."

Without Effort

The art of dance speaks to my soul and spirit. In order to be a good dancer, one needs endurance, flexibility and strength. Gaining these skills does not come easy. It requires hours and hours of practice and passion for expression. Dance, like a great theatrical performance or enthralling book, tells a story with the floor, air and movement of hips, arms and thighs. Dance requires one to reach and extend to the audience, a partner or perhaps the music.

This photo reminds me of another photo of one of my favorite principal dancers, Judith Jamison, who became the Artistic Director for the Alvin Ailey Dance Company. My bestie, Vivian Phillips, had an iconic poster-sized photo of Ms. Jamison in the dining room. I stared at it for what seemed like hours. I was captivated by that long right leg of hers extended without effort, seeming to stretch into oblivion. And her hands—ah… those hands and long fingers that reached for the sky with palms open as though ready to grab something juicy.

In 1997 we went to celebrate the premiere of choreographer George Faison's "Slaves," and we had the opportunity to meet Judith Jamison. I was captivated by her towering height. At 5' 10" her statuesque svelte figure seemed to go on forever. I was disarmed by her charm and grace; I expected pride and haughtiness. She, however, extended her hand with humility and moved like a queen.

Matthew 9:20-21 speaks to my heart: "And a woman who had been suffering from a hemorrhage for twelve years, came up behind Him and touched the fringe of His cloak; for she was saying to herself, 'If I only touch His garment, I will get well.'"

I think about God when I see this photo (and others like the one of Judith Jamison). I linger at photos like this. It's the reach that reminds me that God wants us to reach. When the woman with the issue of blood touched the hem of Christ's garment, she knew something. She was clear enough to know–even in her pain–to reach for Him. He would take care of the rest.

This photo reminds me of the necessity of reaching out with everything you've got. She is extended to her capacity, or at least, I think she is. She leaves me pondering. Perhaps, there is more; more stretch, more height, more pain... Just more... Beyond the reach. What I know for sure is that we must always reach, and sometimes we must reach beyond our capacity.

"Dance is bigger than the physical body. Think bigger than that. When you extend your arm, it doesn't stop at the end of your fingers, because you're dancing bigger than that. You're dancing spirit."

Judith Jameson

Tenderness

This photo says so much about tenderness. I can feel the tenderness with which this man is holding this woman, and I believe that she is his woman. Notice how he kisses her gently on her forehead. They've danced this dance before. They appear to be floating. This photo reminds me that God calls His children gently and tenderly, not forcing Himself on His highest creation.

32

Watch Me

Perhaps he whispered something in her ear as he held her close, something she defied. Or, perhaps he whispered a challenge. He twisted her and she flung away and responded, "Watch me… Watch this. I got this and I don't know how to quit. I will move forward." She stomps and swings her ample hips and owns the space. This photo depicts the essence of dance: skill, beauty, and mastery of the basics. Their form is perfect. Her arms form a flawless balance to the extension of her fingers, and I love those hands. In studying this image, and God's vision for our lives, I reflect on how He wants us to move forward. In one of my favorite devotionals, *God Calling*, it says, "The law of heaven is forward motion." The delicate infusion of the color blue creates an ethereal beauty and contrast just like life itself. Life is not black and white. It's nuanced with so many layers and colors.

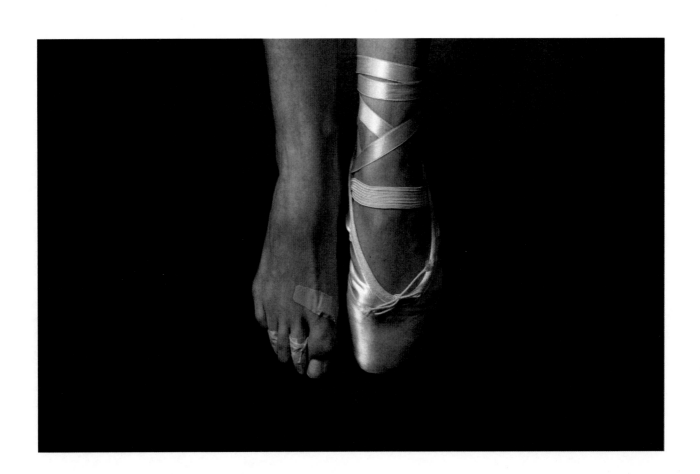

34

Perseverance

The discipline, practice, and perseverance needed to get to toe shoes is staggering. The pain evident in this image blows my hair back. Discipline and perseverance hurts, yet, dancers embrace this journey. Ah… That word, perseverance. I call one of my beloved friends, "My Mary." She is my friend and confidant and I've never met anyone who knows God's Word like Mary. Our conversations are peppered with all things about God. She once said something that I will never forget. "Perseverance and I have always been close, but we haven't consummated the relationship." I never graduated to toe shoes. I wanted to desperately, however, I wasn't willing to do the work. The life lesson I wish to pass on to my children is about the necessity for doing the work. Life offers no shortcuts.

Fifth Position

There are some elements of life that just make us happy; a long embrace, the laughter of our children, the sunrise. And though happiness is important to the soul, I've learned that there is a great difference between happiness and joy. Happiness is dictated by circumstances, by the moment. Joy, on the other hand, is predicated by our position with God. It's okay to want happiness but our yearning should be for joy because it's uninterrupted by life's obstacles. It's not situational. In Galatians 5:22 we have a promise. "But the fruit of the Spirit is love, joy, peace, patience, kindness, goodness, faithfulness."

I Want Happy

I want happy.
I want her
To greet me in the morning
With tulips, hydrangeas and
Cafe au lait
Today—
I want the essence
Of her
Bright yellow dresses
Like the sun
Painted by a grandchild
With the rays
Pointed out
And a big smile
On her face.

I want happy.
I want him
And all he makes me think about
Lace, oceans, gumbo
Gardens and love—lots of love
Today—
I want the smell of coming rain
Even though it's far off
And the woman behind the register
Who said, 'your spirit beckons'
And the man who noticed
My nail polish

"Beautiful on your skin," he said.
I smiled and smiled.

I want happy.
I want them
And freedom from elephants
In rooms and on my chest.
I want good reports
And dreams that come true.

I want to taste happy.
And sip her
Like ice cold lemonade.
And dive into her with a spoon
Into Black Walnut ice cream
And sense the crunch of
Hot water cornbread.

I want to see happy.
Diving, driving, and surviving
And hold butterflies in my hands.
I want to pull her up over my head
When I find sleep.

I want happy.
I want to run with her
For a while
See happy on corners
And in grocery stores.

I want happy.
And I don't want her loosely
I want the embrace
Face to face
The forehead kiss
And sparkle in the touch.
I want happy.
Him
Her
Them
Today
Tomorrow
I want happy.

Leaning In

Captivating, romantic, and sexy. Notice how closely they are aligned. She presses into him as if it's all she has; he holds her softly as if strumming a guitar. Legendary Argentine Flamenco dancer, the late Carlos Gavito said, "The secret of tango is in this moment of improvisation that happens between step and step. It is to make the impossible thing possible: to dance silence. A good dancer is one who listens to the music. We dance the music not the steps."

Together with his longtime partner, Marcela Duran, they created a challenging and dramatic move in which both partners lean in and share an axis. Jorge Luis Borges says, "The tango is a direct expression of something that poets have often tried to state in words: the belief that a fight may be a celebration." Sometimes God prepares us for a fierce battle to take us through the crucible so we can truly understand jubilee. God wants us in alignment. He wants us to share His axis. Life is about the dance.

Instruction

Life is about instruction. When you are ready to receive instruction, it will show up. It's important to posture ourselves in a way that we can hear and act upon sound instruction. God's Word overflows with powerful instructions. God has provided the roadmap for our lives. Proverbs 19:20 says, "Listen to advice and accept instruction, that you may gain wisdom in the future." Psalm 32:8 promises, "I will instruct you and teach you in the way you should go; I will counsel you with my eye upon you." And in Proverbs 4:13 we are commanded, "Keep hold of instruction; do not let go; guard her, for she is your life."

But Now You Own the Day

The world is yours
In spite of raging wars
In your soul
Shattered expectations
Broken pieces
Or dreams that didn't unfold
Still, you own
This day
And the reflection
In the pond
Rippling until sunset.
Sorrow is always unyielding
And pain will buckle bones.

But now…

The time is yours
Even though sand
Passing through
Hour glass portals is hot
And flashes of
Yesterday occupy
Your thoughts.

But now…

The universe is yours
When days are unknown

Heaven says step forward
Even with a broken heart
Unfilled cup
When the vessel is empty
And tenderness
Loses its way.

But now...

The journey is yours—
When paths are unclear
And all you hold tightly
disappears.
Laughter is heard
In every room but yours
And, the plane
That flew into your
Soul
Landed
Abruptly.

But now...

On this day
The world is yours.
This moment belongs to
Only you.
So, laugh
Give joy
Be mercy
Share light

Dance into the twilight.

Now.

Photo Credit: Doraze Legington

Getting to the Skin You're In

Life's intricate path
Will make you trip
Or skip
And the earth will move
While you're making another attempt
At leaping over lightening.
And then arrows will fly
Someone you cherish will
Die
And you will want it all to fade away.
Unworthiness will creep into spaces
That you didn't know existed
And then darkness descends like a blanket
Draped over flowers wilted.

And then something snaps
And you know deeply that
Pregnancy is about pushing through and
Hustling it out.
To get to the mountain top
You must crawl through the valley
Where laughter doesn't exist.
And crumbs of joy
Were devoured before you arrived.

But this life
This path
Is about finding the nectar

The place that God assigned
In all its wonder, glory and pain.
It's about today
This moment
Never to come again
The purpose my friend
Is to find the skin you're in
That precious sweet spot of divinity.
And then—
To live abundantly.

"Dance is the hidden language of the soul."

Martha Graham

54

Calling All Prayer Warriors

There's a battle going on
Around the bend
On the playground
In the corners of the globe
That take you out to battle
The no-second-chances battle
It's *the* battle.

Calling all prayer warriors
Kings, queens, cherubs
Of the bended knee
Righteous spirits
To carry sharpened swords.

Calling the women
Waiting at the well
And with issues of blood
Calling centurions
Bondsmen and
even tax collectors.

It's time to break it down
Like Einstein's fractions
Only the faithful will do
Calling all testimony-carrying warriors
Those-unafraid-to-touch-the-
Hem-of-His-garment warriors
Those who are ready-
To-get-out-of-the-boat warriors
And walk on raging waters.

Calling the men
Real men
To lift some heavy weight
Confident and not confused
Who've picked up their mats
And practiced swinging their swords.
Calling the healers
The teachers and even the poets
With a word or two.

It's battle time
It's battle time
So get some rest.
There's work to do.

Calling all prayer warriors.

Worship the Lord in the beauty of holiness. Dance before Him, all the earth.

1 Chronicles 16:29

You Make Me Want to Dance

When I think of you
I want to dance
A feast of movement
Of exotic fruits and delicacies
In your honor
Oh yes,
Soulful black-eyed peas
And brown sugar sweet potatoes
That make you shimmy
When they reach your tongue.

I want to get on
My tippy toes
Twirl around and around
Dip my hips
Lift my skirt
To my knees and
Shake, shake, shake
I want to dance.

When I think of you
I want to dance
To southern rhythms
Reggae drums
And beats undiscovered
Like your soul.

I want to celebrate your

Vibration and creations
Shaped by your hands.
Pose an arabesque
Over your sentiments
Boogie when you
Weave words of calm
And cradle our children
With love profound

I want to dance.

When I think of you
I want to dance
And proclaim jubilee every day
Move the calendar
Exchange holidays
For a year of dancing.

I want to dance the rumba,
Salsa and strut into spring
With your colors
I want to sway with
Your smile
And tap into your laughter
I want to swing into
Your imagination
And all the joy you bring
I want to waltz
Into the strength of your arms.

I want to dance.

I want to dance until
The earth moves
My feet hurt
My side aches
And sticky sweat takes my hair back
I want to dance
Dance and dance
Until the world knows
Just how great you are.
I want to dance.

Fandango

64

Nothing but Love

Nothing but love
Gathers here and enters
Leaping over
The threshold of more
Love—nothing but love
Lives here and
Wonders, around spaces
Seeking captives
And hearts longing for more
Love
Nothing but love
Abides here
Setting places
At the banquet of mercy
And forgiveness
Nothing but love
Holds hands with
The unlovable
Kisses untouchables
Caresses the forgotten and
Carries the weak and
Invisible
Nothing but love
Arrives here and resides
Reaching for more
Reasons to love
Love more, give more, do more
More love

More love
Love
More
Nothing... but love.

"You dance love, and you dance joy, and you dance dreams. And I know if I can make you smile by jumping over a couple of couches or running through a rainstorm, then I'll be very glad to be a song and dance man…"

Gene Kelly

Chest Stone

It's a small thing
Fist-size
Yet,
Goliath
And his family
Press in and stand
On the aorta
Crushing blood vessels of life
And bone
With force unyielding, this...
Chest stone.
Smothers
And chokes
And reduces life
Hope and spice.
This chest stone
Is un-giving
And unbelieving
Snatching laughter
And light.
It's a small thing
Tea biscuit size
Yet,
It feels like
Boulders and elephants
Tornadoes and typhoons
That press down and
Suck air to

Explode the atmosphere
And heart.
This chest stone
Is a power broker
Offering oppressive
Silence
Retribution
Stares
Bloodshot eyes
And un-love.
Chest stones
Don't love
They occupy
Until rolled away
After the crucifixion
To see
The resurrection.

"Dance when you're broken open. Dance if you've torn the bandage off. Dance in the middle of the fighting… Dance when you're perfectly free."

Jalal al-Din Rumi

That Place

I go to that
Place
Where quiet stills
The heart,
And love
Knows no boundaries.
Love doesn't seek
Without finding
Because love
Knows no depths.
Love is—
It just is.
It is always
Far and wide
Standing between
The years
Of birth and death.
It cries millions
Of tears when children suffer
But never breaks down
Or despairs.
Love champions
Righteousness.

I go to that
Place
Where grace and love wraps
The soul
And covers
With forgiveness

That which in the mind
Cannot be forgiven.
Love shatters
Thoughts and reasoning
And all norms.
And thrusts to
The floor all that
Can't be explained.
Reasons are for
Humanity, but
Love is for God.

I go to that
Place
Where love's hands
Are open
Greeting me with
Peace

"In a society that worships love, freedom, and beauty, dance is sacred. It is a prayer for the future, a remembrance of the past, and a joyful exclamation of thanks for the present."

Amelia Atwater - Rhodes

Love Letter to My Beloved

My Beloved,

Many times, I've asked myself, "Why am I so in love with You?" There are too many reasons to count. However, let me offer just a few. One is because You embrace me with tenderness each and every morning. You never fail me—ever. You greet me with flowers, birds, and beauty incomparable. And, oh yes, the butterflies. You know how much I love butterflies and You allow them to come to me in brilliant colors.

You've given me so many memories and I'm tremendously grateful for each one of them. You were there when I was born, and you saw to it that Doris and Curtis would be my parents. I really believe that they were the only two equipped to care for me, this earth angel of yours with broken wings. I don't know if trumpets blared when I was born, but I think I heard them when you brought my children into the world; safely, with optimum health and so much beauty.

I love You because You love me when I deserve it the least. Even in my obstinacy, pride, rebellion, and when my thinking is wrong and my disobedience glaring—YOU still love me unconditionally. YOU rock me to sleep and catch my tears. YOU hear my crying out and my going within to seek You. YOU are the only one I trust my heart to completely because YOU are the only one who can mend it back together when it's been broken into a million pieces. You've done that for me.

I love YOU because through YOU I have hope for a brighter day no matter how ugly circumstances appear. I know that there is something else going on in another realm. There just has to be—nothing else makes sense. I also know that You're going to have the final Word. I'm finally okay with that… finally.

This love affair has become my life and my yearning. Every single day I'm eager to meet YOU and see what YOU have to say. I'm so glad that YOU know everything about me—YOU are familiar with all of my ways. YOU know when I sit down. YOU, and only YOU, can count the hairs on my head because YOU made me—fearfully and wonderfully.

YOUR mercy is my stepping stone. YOUR grace makes me cry. Could I ever return the love YOU have for me? Is there something I can do? Is there a song, poem, or play I could write to show YOU? I've determined the answer quite simply is no. I cannot imagine the depth of YOUR love and there are no words in Mr. Webster's book to describe it. So, my Beloved, please, allow this letter, this small token to articulate how grateful I am for waking up to YOU and being a part of YOUR world. After all, YOU did create it and everything in it.

Love me some YOU,

Lisa

Singers and dancers alike say, "All my springs are in You."

Psalm 87:7

The Wonder of a Woman

She possesses a signature fragrance
Called light and sunshine
With top notes
Of faith and perseverance.
She brings allure and substance
And exudes dignity.
Her walk is honor.
To pursue the Divine is her wisdom
Grace knows her name.
Yes, Her children rise and call her blessed.
Blessings follow her walk
Tenderheartedness is her talk
She seeks truth for humanity
And searches all understanding.
The Wonder of a Woman
Moves dreams forward
And harnesses resources untold.
From her womb
Life springs forth, cultivates and thrives.
She knows the importance of beginnings
She brings water
From the well of forgiveness
Filling empty and wounded vessels.
Her soul is cast into cauldrons
And her strength tested; burdens laid bare.
She emerges victorious
Drenched in pure gold.
The Wonder of a Woman

Her story is centuries old
She was there at the beginning
When God spoke.
The Holy One called her name—
Woman,
You are a WONDER.

"Life is the dance and you are the dancer."

Eckhart Tolle

Photo Credit: Doraze Legington

84

Heavy

The air is thick
Black smoke occupies the
Space where oxygen
Should be
Your breathing is heavy
With sighs
And weight
Your breath is funky
With heat
And fatigue
Like what your
Eyes say
Every morning
Noon and night.
I'm tired. So tired.
Of the dust
The heavy particles
Choking my tomorrow
I deserve better than this
Heaviness in the atmosphere.
It's heavy.
Too heavy.

Photo Credit: Doraze Legington

Don't Tell Me

For all the women who have suffered physical, emotional or
verbal abuse at the hands or voice of a man who claimed he loved her.

Don't tell me
Just…
Don't tell me
you love me
when you beat me
down
with words or
weeks of silence or
violence
when we stand
on unequally yoked
broken ground
and
unyielding to compromise.

Don't tell me
Just…
Don't tell me
you love me
when you disfigure
my face
and
you place
my spirit
under your feet,
feet so much bigger
than mine.

Don't tell me

Just...
Don't tell me
you love me
raising your hands
to my ideas
breaking my teeth and limbs
and
crushing my identity
and
all the good I
believed about me
as you destroy me
while uplifting you
and punching with words
so vile
that will take me
a lifetime to dislodge
and
side stepping my longing
for peace
with an uppercut
to my jaw.

Don't tell me
Just...
Don't tell me
you love me
when sleep eludes
and blood exudes
from open sores
and
a closed fist
to my heart

Just...
Don't tell me
as I struggle
for breath
and life.
breath...
and...
life...

Fondu

The Sun Rises in South Africa

Breathtaking...
The original sun
Rising in the
Original east
Tucked behind
God's canvas
Of blue and melon.
Its brilliance beckons me
To sing, dance,
Whisper.
Gazelles sit in
Anticipation
Wisdom quiets the
Wind and rivers become
Motionless at this spectacle
Of sheer brilliance.
Everyday...
Even when unseen,
A promise exists
And His paintbrush
Touches the canvas
To steal my breath again.
Rising in the
Original east
Tucked behind unlimited
Boundaries and splashes of
Pink, purple, and gold.
And in that moment
I am still
And awakened

In this land of all beginnings.
I watch with wonder
As flamingos gaze
Impalas halt
Clouds gather for
The symphony and
The original Conductor
And Master Artist
Takes His place—
In this land of all beginnings.
The music reaches a crescendo
And all creation
Stands silent while
The original sun
Rises in the
Original east
In the land of all beginnings.

"It is music and dancing that makes me at peace with the world and at peace with myself."

Nelson Mandela

Believe

You must believe
You must stand tall
You must know in your heart
Of hearts
God has it all—
In the palm of His hands
You reside without walls
All your issues are
Resolved
According to His Will
God has it all—
You must believe
Please have resolve
You must know in your soul of souls
God has it all—
Even with all the noise
And doubt
That keeps screaming out
The prognosis from man
The quicksand and the pain
The heartbreak and the rain
When the people who say you can't,
Remember God says you can.
He wants us to place our hands in His
Renew our confidence
And go to the mountaintop
Jump off the cliff without a frown
Knowing God will build our wings

On the way down.
You must believe
You must believe
It is so
You must believe.

"You dance because you have to. Dance is an essential part of life that has always been with me."

Katherine Dunham

Suddenly

Suddenly,
There was nothing.
No ideas
Imagination
Thoughtfulness
Consideration
No light
Or rays of light
Only—darkness.
No kisses
Or attraction
No deliciousness
Holding hands
Soft embraces
Gentle spirit
Or wonder.
There wasn't even
Silence—
That too was interrupted
By meaningless
Ripples of noise.

Suddenly,
The music stopped.
And angels
Refused to sing.
Sweetness departed
Grace vanished
And love

Closed its door.
Laughter couldn't be found
Joy was gone
And tender embraces
Of a passionate tango
Were unwelcome.
The applause left.
Erotica couldn't be found
And mountains
Climbed in togetherness
Crumbled.

Oceans once greeted
With open palms
Were no longer visited
And conversations
Once spirited and
Alive became
Lifeless sentences—
Giving way to two
And three
Syllable words.
Hello
Goodbye
Nice day
It's raining
It's midnight.
And,
The tearing of souls
Lasts until morning
And quiet footsteps

Once welcomed
Become thunder.

Suddenly,
Masks turn into
Dust
And the naked
Spirit reveals
Truths embarked by pain
And remembrances
Love—
Once cherished
With arms open wide
Folded into
Yesterday.
Suddenly.

God, Is That You?

Good morning. Thanks for waking me up again and placing my feet on the floor. Thank you for opening yet another door and allowing me to walk, talk and see. In the mirror—my smile, brown eyes and slightly crooked teeth—the reflection is You in me. Your perfection shines through my imperfections, reminding me of life's possibilities. Good morning.

God, is that You? As angels whisper, holy, holy, holy. Is that You calling my name and breathing on me, in me? Is that You waiting for me? Waiting for me to be still so I can know You are who You say You are? Waiting for me to catch my breath so I can take in Yours?

God, is that You? Is that You trying to get my attention? Is it You who made me rise with Your sun so I will always remember Your Son? Is it You who taught me how to walk again and stand straight? Is it You who put this swing in my hips and pen in my hand so I could fiercely tell the world about You?

God, is that You? Is that Your gentle breeze and kaleidoscope of colors? Is it Your paintbrush that strokes the sky at dusk with hues that fold into night? Is it Your music I hear? Are these Your dreams in my head and Your heart that I'm in? Is it Your love and peace that I enter, always on time?

God, is that You? Is it You that bends my knees and catches each and every tear? Is it You that takes my fears and discards them with yesterday's trash? Is it You who bears my pain and takes my rusty, dusty, half-baked excuses and still allows me to see truth, bear witness to mercy, and experience the mosaic of Your joy?

God, is that You? Is it really You showering me with grace like gentle rain and piercing my heart with bolts of thunder? Is it You giving me another mountain and signing me up for yet another Master's class to learn Your path and lean again on Your mighty shoulders? Is it You welcoming me to majesty?

Good morning. Of course, it's You. Please, come in.

To the Artist

Where would I
Be
Without you?
Lost
Without your room
Full of love
And colors and layers of more love.
I can't survive
Without your
Words.
I can't exist
Without your
Reflections and light
Tap shoes and
Heights galore to which
You take me.

Where would I
Be
Without you?
Lost
In another space
Conflicted
Without your brilliant
Divine Workmanship.

Where would I
Be

Without you?
Lost
Without your music and melodies
When I greet each
Morning with song.
I need the key of G
Like flowers need air.
Collaborating with wood
And earth's metals
Is not an option for
My soul
I have to have
All of it.

Where would I
Be
Without you?
Your thoughts
Pens and paintbrushes
Pianos and lacquer
Stones and chisel
Carvings and canvas
Enamel and glass
And threads that weave
Stories?

Lost
In an unending span
Of
Uninterrupted darkness
Devoid of truth.

Jeté

The Price of Oil in the Alabaster Box

No one knows the price
or years of yearning and pain
or struggles and climbing
in vain
no one knows about the boulders
broken
and bones chipped
to pour the elixir,
the fragrant oil
of wonder and anointing.

From Lebanon's cedars
An oil of myrrh
Poured graciously to purify
The most vile and contemptible
The proud and despicable.

No one knows the price
or rivers of tears
or millions of prayers on
bloody and worn-out knees
the warrior's stance—
to produce and pour
from the Alabaster box
the elixir
the priceless oil
from the soul's reservoir.

From the holy heart
The oil of myrrh
Released from the spirit
To free
And sanctify
The hopeless.

No one knows the price
or years of loneliness
walking through Samaria
or staring into darkness
opening hell's gates.
No one knows the price
of the strides uphill
with vessels of water
and bare feet that can't suffice
and finding the lake empty
and the soul parched
longing for dewdrops
in yet another desert.

No one knows the price
of life
or the stretching and
God's balm
His unseen treasures
the Spirit's anointing
for the oil
in the alabaster box.

And David danced before the Lord with all his might; and David was wearing a linen ephod.

2 Samuel 6:14

Sing Me a Song, Sweet Honey

Dedicated to *Sweet Honey in the Rock*

Sing me a song,
Sweet Honey
Take me to distant
Shores and
Then bring me
Home.

Sing me to the sweet spot
Of grace
Sing about grit and grits
And my glorious, coarse
Roots.

Sing me awake
And to sleep
Quiet my restless spirit.

Sing me a song,
Sweet Honey
About freedom
And charity
And love.

Sing me a song,
Sweet Honey
Take me to revolutions
And sacred paths
Of forgiveness.

Take me to our
Strength.

Sing to me your
Wisdom and
The sweet
Honey pot
Of your soul.

"Making dances is an act of progress; it is an act of growth, an act of music, an act of teaching, an act of celebration, an act of joy."

Alvin Ailey

You are Flowers

(For Jade and Heaven)

Like the gardenias in Billie's hair
And deep purple of Alice's vision
You are the flowers I love.
The bouquet—
Multitudes of vibrant colors
The sunshine yellow of daffodils
The candy apple red of azaleas
The bold purple of orchids in bloom
And passion pink in tulips,
You are the flowers
Of my life
The lushness of tropical palms
Before and after rain.
I love to be greeted by you
Every day
And surrounded by your richness.
Look up
Look up
Flowers always look up
To say hello to Master Creator
You are flowers.

My Heroes

My heroes created songs...
Bebop, bebop...
Bebop, bebop...
Lady sings the blues
With strings and borrowed trumpets
Their genius reined
At humanity's denial
Bringing the world jazz.
Satchmo birthed the model
The Count never failed
Our master of irresistible swing...
Rat-a-tat-tat...
Rat-a-tat-tat
Syncopated and highly precise
My heroes created songs...
Round midnight...
Round midnight
The Titans
Miles, The Duke, Lionel,
Wes, Thelonious, Coleman, Parker,
Coltrane,
Ella, Sarah, and Dizzy—
Honey-hued Harlem gurus
Cooked, grooved, composed
Brilliant harmonies
Curling phrases
Uncluttered innovation
My heroes created songs

Dropping ice cubes of majestic sound...
In silence
Delivering intimacy and passion
Perfection, commanding, gifted...
Skeet-da-da-da...
Skeet-da-da-da
My heroes created music
Of life's experiences
And rich apprenticeships.
My heroes gave the world
Jazz.

"I don't remember not dancing. When I realized I was alive and these were my parents, and I could walk and talk, I could dance."

Gregory Hines

Photo Credit: Doraze Legington

Serenity Now

I seek you, Serenity
I want you now.
I will not wait.
No, not another moment.
I can taste You
And hear your
Sweet,
Sweet
Voice.

You will not elude me.
Daily I will search
Until I find You
My place of
Everlasting peace.
That space of listening
And hearing the
Melody
Of still
Still
Serenity
Now.

I will reach for You
And You alone
No matter what
Comes my way
Or
How long noise stays.

Mambo

Photo Credit: Dee Hunter-Smith

For my sons, Biron, Kimon, and Josh;
and our grandsons, Jackson, Kyle, Jamal and Li'l John.
In memory of the sons who've lost their lives to gun violence and
oppressive police policies: Trayvon Martin, Alton Sterling, Stephon Clark,
Philando Castile, Walter Scott, Eric Harris, Tony Robinson Jr.,
Rumain Brisbon, Tamir Rice, Laquan McDonald, Michael Brown,
Eric Garner, Jordan Edwards, and Botham Jean.

Be Alive: I Want You to Live

Live.
Please—I beg you.
I want you
To live.
I want to bask
In your person
In your fire
And see you arrive
Walk through the
Door and bring
The outdoors
On you—
I want you to thrive
In your person
Your God-given,
Life-affirming talents and gifts.

I want to see you
Get out of the car
And run and get my sugah
And eat sweet potato pie

And shrimp salad
From the table
I want to see the
Manifestation of your dreams—
Rockstar
Astronaut
Literary genius
Mr. President

Read those scriptures to me
Out loud.

Live.
Baby, please.
I want you
To live.
And create
A world
Without hate
Or bullets that
Rip through torsos
Destroying
Everything.

Live.
I want you
To live.
And grasp life by both hands
And squeeze and squeeze and squeeze
Bringing life
And lemonade
Peace and serenity
Compassion and grace
Mercy baby—
I need to see your FACE
I must see your dignity
In this place
In every place.

Live.
I want you
To live.
I need to see

The love in your eyes
So you can give
So you can BE
All that God intended
You to Be

So...
LIVE.

Words to This Poem

I will find words
To this poem
Behind a desk
Or under a rug.
I will look behind
Ears and in
Buried treasure.
I will search
Beyond rainbows
Songs and my music.
I will find the words
To this poem.
I will search
The stairwells
Gardens of hope
And inside an
Erupting volcano.
I will find words
In between days
And at the end
Of storms
I will find words
I will find the words
To this poem.

134

Viv's Table of Joy

To receive an invitation to sit at the table is exclusive because the feast includes a delectable entrée fit for royalty. Only those minds that seek answers, solve problems, and minister to souls, are invited. Sometimes, too, invitations are sent to those whose cups are empty and whose nerves are frayed. I even heard about those being invited who needed a kick in the derrière. My soul was always nurtured there, and a vessel invariably offered to catch my tears.

In life's call there are buried treasures hidden underneath the vibrant tablecloth and whispered secrets only the peach cobbler knows… gone so long ago. Wisdom abounded, along with passion, compassion, accountability, integrity and love. And I was never turned away no matter what was going on. Whether the gathering was impromptu or planned for days, I always had a place setting.

I traveled from distant places and through time zones to get to my spot at the table. It was there that rich butter pound cakes and succulent collards welcomed me. Cheap wine and expensive champagne were our elixirs as we listened to bass guitars rumble in the background. There were many, many moments when we got up and danced because the rhythm of the banquet called for the immediate movement of our limbs. There I was reminded that only God delivers joy. It's one of His many promises. Happiness depends on happenings, but joy is everlasting—if claimed. And this table of joy is God's gift to those of us who are invited to partake—generous grace to myself and all who would receive it.

At the table of joy plays are written, dreams conceived, public policy created, children hugged, and culture and art validated. At this place being is appreciated. Just being—real, sweet, obnoxious, funky, ethereal, irreverent, visceral, quiet, tender—as you are. Nothing was off limits for discussion; one could be crucified or verified. Our conversations were rich. The topics explored range from recipes, to racism, to global warming, to the accoutrements police have to abuse the law. At the table we sliced and diced. Great artists were honored, loved ones buried, marriages restored, and children born. At Viv's table of joy, love reigned abundantly without condemnation or judgment.

Afterward, there was fulfillment; once-empty vessels overflowed. There is a sense of inspiration and encouragement. I left the table with a sense of peace and tranquility. I was reassured that yes, one more step was needed, or more salt, or spice, or perhaps even more brokenness or pruning was required. I folded my napkin, thankful for the tablespoon of renewed sanity. I can move forward now fiercely, fight on courageously and break down a few barriers boldly.

"My body is very different from most of the dancers I dance with. My hair is different than most I dance with. But I didn't let that stop me. Black girls rock and can be ballerinas."

Misty Copeland

Prayers at the Wall

(Written after my trip to Israel)

I prayed for you
At the wall
With Holy steps
I took it all
Issues of heart
And mind
Asked for life's direction
So hard to find.
I prayed for you
At the wall
Straight to the throne
A room meant
For you
I wrote your
Name on torn yellow paper
And squeezed it
In between
King Herod's stones
Now, you will
Never feel alone.
I prayed for you
At the wall
For you to hear
When the trumpets blow
And God calls.

Pointe

I AM NOT a nigga

I AM NOT a nigga
I AM NOT a
hoochie, coon, spade, niggress
OR ANY SUCH
term that describes
articulates, punctuates
my being
my soul
my rhythm
my essence—
this breath and name of mine
birthed
by the Creator
before the beginning
of time—No,
I AM NOT a nigga.

I AM NOT a nigga
I AM NOT less than
scum
nor will I
be treated like a bum
or trash
or foul droppings
while my ancestors'
ashes, dust, bare knuckles
and broken bones
remain buried under the sea.

I AM NOT a nigga
I AM NOT deprived
worthless, hedonistic,
lazy or crazy
not grinning,
shucking or jiving.

I represent my life
my momma
and momma's momma
the lives of those courageous
unnamed souls
at the bottom of
the Atlantic
who would rather die
than live oppressed.
I give my life—
Like my daddy's daddy tilled the soil
And read by candlelight
At death's door.

They called me nigga
as I gave birth again
aboard a filthy vessel
surrounded by
huge rats
gnawing through wood
and wombs.
They called us niggas
at the shrieks of
our friends
our eyes fixated at

the horror of the living
chained to the decaying
Yet...
they called us niggas?

They called us niggas
as our aunts and uncles
jumped overboard
rather than endure
anymore
Any more.
And the sharks encircled
again
and again
and again
Still...
they called us niggas.

They called me nigga
as I laid in the sun
after the lash
met my flesh
forty times forty
and my bones were exposed
from the tearing
of my mahogany humanity.

They called us niggas
as we pounded the
fields
and the sun
incinerated our backs
and our children

left in a pig's trough
could not suckle.
Then, the rains came—
unrelenting storms poured
wrath at sin
and each baby
no more than six months
drowned
by the waters—
and our tears.
Thirty of us
thirty of them
swallowed by swollen waters
so they wouldn't be
called niggas
like we were
as we wailed and grieved.

They called me nigga wench
as I was shoved from
auction to auction
my breasts buttered
with palm oil
like any animal
at market.
They called us niggas
while they snuffed out our lights
and chained our souls
blew up our homes
lynched our families
dismembered our limbs
and castrated our manhood

with the castration of
oppression
setting fires to our ideas
and dreams.

How confused you must be
to think this wretched word
defines me—
I AM NOT a nigga
I AM NOT yo nigga
a nigga
their nigga
her nigga
his nigga
I AM NOT
a
nigga

People

There are certain people who
Bring fuel to the fire
Others take oxygen out of the air
And some shock the system.
Cemeteries are full of hopes,
Despair, disrepair, and salt—
It just is that people are people
With arms and legs
Some, not so much.
There are some souls who
Are hungry with passion or desire
And okay with not knowing it all
And being all to everyone and everybody
Because they are people
Who bring their flaws,
Ashy legs and all but
They don't poison the space.
There are people who
Change the game
Make new rules and
Transform lives
And those who are blood suckers
Waiting to take what
Doesn't belong to them.
Some people belong to life
And give life
Holding it gently with both hands
Others strangle it and bear
Strange fruit.

The Artists

LaWonda "La'Hunter" Hunter-Smith (page 128) is a Washington D.C. native and Dallas Fort Worth resident since 1989. La 'Hunter started her dance training at the age of two, learning authentic African dance styles with Melvin Deale's African Heritage of Dancers and Drummers. She learned how to command a stage with Carol Foster's DC Youth Ensemble and became a proud member of Mike Malone's Everyman Street Theatre. La'Hunter was trained extensively at the Duke Ellington School of the Arts and studied under world-famous ballerina Sandra Fortune-Green. La'Hunter was a lead soloist with the Dallas Black Dance Theatre, and worked with master choreographers like Alonzo King, Blondell Cummings, and Gene Hill Sagan. She is a past choreographer with the Soul Rep Theatre Company, and a Professional Division and advanced modern staff member at the Fort Worth campus of Texas Ballet Theater School. La 'Hunter was most recently nominated for five Irma P. Hall Black Theater Awards and was awarded two for Best Musical and Best Scenic Design for a Musical.

Michelle Gibson (pages 50, 84, 86, 124) is a choreographer, Cultural Ambassador, educator, and performing artist. Michelle received her Bachelor of Fine Art in Dance from Tulane University and her Master of Fine Art in Dance from Hollins University/American Dance Festival at Duke University. Michelle is a nine-year faculty member with the American Dance Festival's three, and six-week school intensive held at Duke University. She taught and set choreography at various intensives, institutions and universities including, but not limited to, Middlebury College, Spelman College, and Henderson State University. Michelle has also choreographed for several theater companies and live entertainment organizations locally and across the country.

Michelle's choreographic works range from genres of the African Diaspora, Afro and Contemporary Modern, Afro Funk, Jazz, and her own New Orleans Second Line Aesthetic.

As a candidate for the Katherine Dunham Technique Certification, Michelle traveled to Rennes, France, sharing her New Orleans Second Aesthetics as a Guest Lecturer at the Compagnie Engrenage.

About the Author

Poet, essayist, playwright and lover of God's Word, *Lisa Brown Ross* is an award-winning writer who is a lover of dance, music, theatre and poetry and a seeker of wisdom, peace and justice. Her career spans radio and television reporting, public relations and public affairs consulting, motivational speaking and leadership development. Lisa began her career as a radio reporter and freelanced for the Associated Press, National Public Radio, ABC Radio and Satellite News. She served for more than 12 years as a chief spokesperson for the Immigration and Naturalization Service in Houston, Texas and Washington, DC, and later as Public Affairs Director for the Seattle Police Department.

Lisa has served as a guest editor for Society Life Magazine, Theater Jones Magazine and ibelieve.com. She is the author of *Red Beans, Rice and Chopstix Too; Sapphires and Satin Beauty of Black Soul;* and "The MAAFA; A Commemoration of the Transatlantic Slave Trade."

By White House appointment, Lisa served on the strategic planning team for the Economic Summit of Industrialized Nations where she managed more than 2,000 international media organizations and designed a process to document minority-owned participation in the Summit's hiring process. She worked for the National Council of Negro Women, Inc. as executive producer for the organization's 50th anniversary television show and wrote resolutions for African Heads-of-State for an international conference in Zimbabwe, South Africa.

In 2004 Lisa and her husband, John founded the LJR Group, Inc., a public affairs and public relations consulting agency. The organization was responsible for providing all communication assets for the USAID's educational efforts on the continent of Africa. Before founding the LJR Group, Inc. she served as Leadership Programs Director for the Robert Wood Johnson Foundation's Urban Health Initiative.

"My heart's desire is to create a space of healing and to roll out the red carpet for God's Word."

Made in the USA
Middletown, DE
08 June 2020